Shih Tzu

Lion Dog

by Joyce Markovics

Consultant: Jo Ann White
Author of *The Official Book of the Shih Tzu*
Past President, American Shih Tzu Club

BEARPORT
PUBLISHING

New York, New York

Credits

Cover and Title Page, © Paulette Braun/Pets by Paulette; TOC, © Eric Isselée/Shutterstock; 4, Courtesy of the Doehrman family; 5L, Courtesy of the Doehrman family; 5R, © Erin G. Edwards; 6L, © Miao Liao/Shutterstock; 6R, © Les Palenik/Shutterstock; 7, Courtesy of the Doehrman family; 8L, © John Daniels/Ardea; 8R, © Sara Robinson/Shutterstock; 9, © Bildarchiv Preussischer Kulturbesitz/Art Resource, NY; 10, © The Art Gallery Collection/Alamy; 11, © Hutchinson's Popular and Illustrated Dog Encyclopedia, ca. 1934, Courtesy of Victor Joris; 12, © Barcroft/Fame Pictures; 13, © Monika Graff/The Image Works; 14, © Paulette Braun/Pets by Paulette; 15, © Jochem Wijnands/Picture Contact/Alamy; 16T, © Olivier Digoit/Alamy; 16B, © Gina Callaway/Shutterstock; 17L, © Ruth Fremson/The New York Times/Redux; 17R, © Nancy Tobin/WomenSetSail LLC; 18, © Geri Lavrov/ Photographer's Choice/Getty Images; 19T, © AP Images/Hobbs News Sun/Kimberly Ryan; 19B, © Paulette Braun/Pets by Paulette; 20, Courtesy of Kevin & Norma Wright; 21, © C. Steimer/Arco Images GmbH/Alamy; 22L, © Thierry Grun/Alamy; 22R, © Thierry Grun/Alamy; 23, © Connie Summers/Paulette Johnson/Fox Hill Photo; 24, © Lisa Sheridan/Studio Lisa/Hulton Archive/Getty Images; 25L, © Michael Parkinson/Camera Press/ Retna Ltd.; 25R, © AsiaPix/Alamy; 26, © Lucas Jackson/Reuters/Landov; 27, © Robin Nelson/Photo Edit; 28, © pixel-pets/Shutterstock; 29, © Robert Dowling/Corbis; 29TL, © Anne Kitzman/Shutterstock; 31, © Eric Isselée/ Shutterstock; 32, © Eric Isselée/Shutterstock.

Publisher: Kenn Goin
Senior Editor: Lisa Wiseman
Creative Director: Spencer Brinker
Original Design: Dawn Beard Creative
Photo Researcher: Amy Dunleavy

Library of Congress Cataloging-in-Publication Data

Markovics, Joyce L.
  Shih tzu : lion dog / by Joyce Markovics.
    p. cm. — (Little dogs rock II)
  Includes bibliographical references and index.
  ISBN-13: 978-1-936088-19-5 (library binding)
  ISBN-10: 1-936088-19-3 (library binding)
  1. Shih tzu—Juvenile literature. I. Title.
  SF429.S64M37 2011
  636.76—dc22
                    2010006245

For more information, write to Bearport Publishing Company, Inc., 101 Fifth Avenue, Suite 6R, New York, New York 10003. Printed in the United States of America in North Mankato, Minnesota.

062010
042110CGB

10 9 8 7 6 5 4 3 2 1

Contents

A Four-Legged Helper

The Doehrmans' new Shih Tzu (SHEED ZOO) was no ordinary pet. Georgie was a **service dog** that the family got to help their son, Alex, who has autism.

Almost immediately, three-year-old Alex bonded with Georgie—a friendly, outgoing ball of fur. "He never let her down," remembers Alex's dad. From the first day on, Georgie and Alex were inseparable.

▲ **Six-year-old Alex with his mom and Georgie**

Autism is a serious medical **disorder** that affects the brain and the way people communicate, form relationships, and behave. As many as 1 in 110 children in the United States have some form of autism.

Soon, incredible things began happening. Before meeting Georgie, Alex was unable to talk. However, within months of Georgie's arrival, Alex began speaking. He didn't just say a word or two. "Alex was talking in sentences," said his mom. Alex's parents were amazed! They knew that Georgie's relationship with Alex had helped bring about this change in their son.

Shih Tzus make great service ▶ dogs because of their willingness to please and to learn.

▲ **Georgie's small size and soft black-and-white fur made her a perfect cuddling buddy.**

A Lifelong Friendship

Over the next 14 years, Georgie and Alex grew even closer. Each day after school, the little dog greeted Alex at the door, licking him all over. At bedtime, Alex's autism made him restless. So Georgie slept next to him to help him fall asleep.

chrysanthemum

Shih Tzus are sometimes called "**chrysanthemum**-faced dogs." The way the hair on their round faces grows in different directions reminds people of the way petals grow on a chrysanthemum flower.

▲ **The Shih Tzu is known for its "pushed-in" face and its soft, warm expression.**

Georgie also helped Alex in other ways. When Alex had trouble paying attention, the little dog bumped his leg to keep him alert. Georgie also watched over Alex when he was home alone, making sure he knew when the phone rang or when the smoke alarm went off. Georgie was more than a dog—she was the best **companion** Alex could have hoped for.

▲ **The Doehrman family is thankful for Georgie's help. Sadly, Georgie passed away in 2009.**

Palace Pets

Georgie's companionship is typical of a Shih Tzu. These small, loving dogs have been prized as house pets for more than a thousand years. Some historians believe that this **breed** got its start in ancient Tibet and was then brought to China. The Chinese named the dog *Shih Tzu*, meaning "lion." Why? Some people thought the Shih Tzu, with its long, flowing hair, looked like a tiny lion.

▲ Lions are considered to be very important animals in Chinese culture. Since some people think that Shih Tzus resemble lions, the dogs have always been treasured by the people of China.

Shih Tzus were first raised in China by **royal** families. During the **Ming dynasty** (1368—1644), rulers and other important people kept them as companions in their palaces. These royal dogs were treasured by their owners, and selling them was considered a crime.

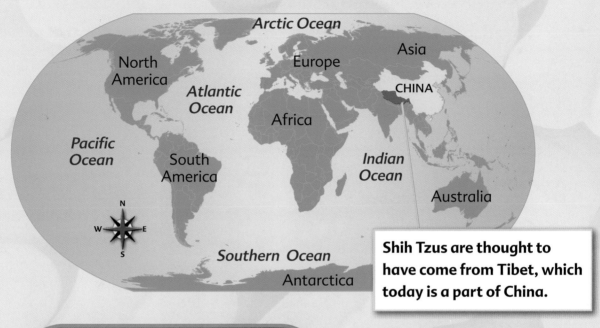

Arctic Ocean

North America

Atlantic Ocean

Europe

Asia

CHINA

Africa

Pacific Ocean

South America

Indian Ocean

Australia

Southern Ocean

Antarctica

N W E S

Shih Tzus are thought to have come from Tibet, which today is a part of China.

◀ The Chinese sometimes referred to Shih Tzus as "under-the-table dogs" because their bodies are so low to the ground that they can fit easily under a table.

The Shih Tzu is mentioned in Chinese writings that date back to the 14th century.

The Empress's New Pups

In the 1800s, a Chinese empress named Cixi (tsuh-SHEE) was so fond of the little dogs that she kept a **kennel** of them. She raised many dogs over her lifetime. After she died in 1908, her kennel was shut down and few Shih Tzus were **bred** in China. The little lion dogs almost became **extinct**.

◀ **Empress Cixi was a powerful ruler who took pleasure in raising her beloved dogs.**

All the Shih Tzus in the world today can be traced back to 13 of the empress's dogs—seven females and six males.

Luckily, a few of the dogs that survived were sent to England and Scandinavia. There, they became more and more popular. Starting in the late 1930s, American soldiers stationed in Europe decided to bring the **regal** little dogs back home with them.

▲ **Shih Tzus in England in the 1930s**

Solid and Sturdy

Since the 1950s, Shih Tzus have continued to gain popularity in the United States. Year after year, they rank in the list of the top ten most popular dog breeds, according to the **American Kennel Club**. What draws many people to this friendly breed is the dogs' small size.

◀ **Since Shih Tzus are so small, they can easily travel around with their owners.**

A Shih Tzu is considered a "toy dog"—the name of a group that is made up of several small dog breeds. Other toy breeds include the Chinese crested, the Maltese, the Italian greyhound, the Pomeranian, and the Yorkshire terrier.

Just under one foot (30 cm) tall, Shih Tzus are small but solid. They weigh from 9 to 16 pounds (4 to 7 kg). Along with their small size, Shih Tzus are known for their elegant **carriages**. With their heads held high and their tails curved over their backs, they move so smoothly that they appear to float.

Shih Tzus often look as if they are floating on air when they walk.

Colorful Coats

Besides their small size and elegant carriages, Shih Tzus are also recognized for their beautiful **coats**, which come in a rainbow of colors. Some have coats that are silver and white or **brindle** and white. Others are just one color such as red, black, gold, or silver. Their coats may be smooth or slightly wavy. All Shih Tzus have one thing in common, though—soft, silky hair that grows very long.

▲ **A gold Shih Tzu (left), a black Shih Tzu (middle), and a silver and white Shih Tzu (right)**

The long hair on a Shih Tzu's face can sometimes get in the dog's way. Many owners choose to trim it short or tie it up. This helps the dog to see better and prevents the hair from irritating its large, sensitive eyes.

Shih Tzus usually have a double coat. This means that they have two kinds of hair. The undercoat is soft and tangles easily, especially on older puppies. The outer coat is long and stronger than the undercoat.

▲ Some Shih Tzus have a special hairdo called a topknot. To make one, the hair around the dog's eyes is carefully brushed, pulled back, and tied with a bow.

Grooming

Grooming a Shih Tzu's long beautiful coat is one of the most important responsibilities owners have. Since its hair tangles easily and often collects leaves and dirt from the ground, the dog must be brushed daily. Some owners don't have time to do this, so they give their pets puppy cuts—short haircuts that are easy to care for.

▲ **A Shih Tzu getting its long hair brushed**

A Shih Tzu with a puppy cut ▶

Besides brushing, Shih Tzus also need to have their hair washed every three weeks. Owners use a gentle shampoo and some even use a blow-dryer to quickly dry their pets' hair.

In addition to hair care, a Shih Tzu's toenails should be clipped every other week. Long nails can be painful and make it hard for a dog to walk. Clipping can be done at home or by a **veterinarian**.

A Shih Tzu getting a bath

All dogs, including Shih Tzus, may have **dewclaws**. These are extra toenails located higher up on the dog's leg.

▲ **A dewclaw on a Shih Tzu**

Healthy and Happy

A Shih Tzu that is well cared for will usually live a long life. To keep these little dogs healthy, owners should walk them daily. They don't need as much exercise as larger dogs, but they still need some. They also must not be overfed. Too much food can lead to them becoming overweight and unhealthy.

Shih Tzus generally live from 11 to 15 years—much longer than most big dogs. Some have lived for as long as 18 years!

▲ When taking a walk, it's always best for an owner to keep his or her pet on a leash so it doesn't run into the street and get hurt.

Regular trips to the veterinarian are a must for Shih Tzus. These little dogs are known to suffer from eye and kidney problems. They need shots to help keep them disease-free.

Just like people, Shih Tzus can get gum disease. To prevent it, the little dogs should have their teeth cleaned by their owners or their veterinarians regularly.

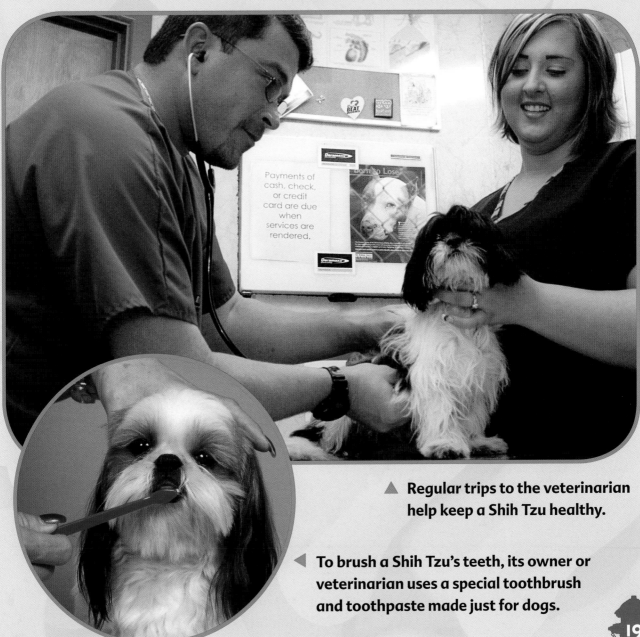

▲ Regular trips to the veterinarian help keep a Shih Tzu healthy.

◀ To brush a Shih Tzu's teeth, its owner or veterinarian uses a special toothbrush and toothpaste made just for dogs.

A Huge Personality

Shih Tzus are cheerful, outgoing, and affectionate. They love to be the center of attention and to be around people. They tend to become very attached to their human family. For example, Gizmo and Freeway go everywhere with their owners Kevin and Norma. Even when Kevin and Norma travel around on their motorcycle, the "boys," as Kevin calls them, ride in a **sidecar**.

▲ **Kevin and Norma adopted Gizmo (right) and Freeway (left) from an animal shelter.**

A Shih Tzu's love of attention makes it a great performer. Some compete with other dogs in special **agility** contests. Others have even been trained to dance with their owners. This is called **canine freestyle**. The dogs learn simple steps to perform to music with their human dance partners.

▲ **A Shih Tzu running through an agility course**

During agility contests, the dogs jump over bars, run through tunnels, and weave in and out of poles.

Puppies

All puppies are little, but Shih Tzu puppies are extremely tiny. Most of them weigh between three to five ounces (85 to 142 g), and are about the size of a hamster. A female usually has three to four puppies in a **litter**, though she may have more. The puppies feed on their mother's milk during the first eight weeks of their lives.

◀ **A sleepy seven-day-old pup**

▲ **Seven-day-old pups getting milk from their mother**

A Shih Tzu puppy is delicate and should be handled gently. Its entire body should be supported when it's being lifted or carried.

After they are **weaned**, Shih Tzu pups should be taught basic manners, such as not to nip, jump, or go to the bathroom inside the house. Encouraging good behavior early on will help puppies learn how to become well-behaved adults.

An owner training his dog to stay.

Famous Pooches

As in ancient China, some royal familes in the 20th century kept Shih Tzus as companions. In 1933, the British Royal family received a pet Shih Tzu, named Choo-Choo, from Queen Maud of Norway. Princess Elizabeth, who later became Queen Elizabeth II, and her sister Princess Margaret loved spending time with the little dog.

▲ **Princess Elizabeth (right) with Choo-Choo and her sister Margaret**

Today, some very famous people keep Shih Tzus as pets, too. For example, billionaire Bill Gates, founder of the computer technology company Microsoft, owns a Shih Tzu named Ballmer. Also, the singer Mariah Carey was given twin Shih Tzu puppies, Bing and Bong, while on tour in Japan.

▲ Bill Gates

Actress Elizabeth Taylor has had many pet dogs, including a Shih Tzu.

▲ Elizabeth Taylor and her Shih Tzu

The Right Fit

Shih Tzus are not just pets for famous people. This ancient breed can be the perfect pet for almost anyone. Whether **show dogs** or **lapdogs**, they delight their owners and their love of people makes them truly wonderful companions.

Every year, the American Shih Tzu Club holds a big show. Shih Tzus from all over the country compete against one another to be named **Best in Show**!

▲ **A Shih Tzu show dog**

All dogs, even little ones, are a big responsibility, however. Shih Tzus need a lot of care and attention. Yet for the person who is willing to devote the necessary time and energy, these proud tiny lion dogs can bring their owners a lifetime of smiles!

The bond that a Shih Tzu shares with its young owner is very strong.

Shih Tzus at a Glance

Weight:	9–16 pounds (4–7 kg)
Height at Shoulder:	9–10.5 inches (23 cm–26.7 cm)
Coat Hair:	Usually have a double coat; long, soft silky hair
Colors:	Some are silver and white or brindle and white; others are just one color such as red, black, gold, or silver
Area of Origin:	Tibet
Life Span:	11 to 15 years or more
Personality:	Happy, alert, loyal

Best in Show

What makes a great Shih Tzu? Every owner knows that his or her dog is special. Judges in dog shows, however, look very carefully at a Shih Tzu's appearance and behavior. Here are some of the things they look for:

Behavior: should be lively, alert, and affectionate

short, square muzzle

tail curved over the back

large, heavily coated ears

long flowing coat

Glossary

agility (uh-JIL-uh-tee) the ability to move fast and easily

American Kennel Club (uh-MER-i-kuhn KEN-uhl KLUHB) a national organization that is involved in many activities having to do with dogs, including collecting information about dog breeds, registering purebred dogs, and setting rules for dog shows

Best in Show (BEST IN SHOH) the top-rated dog in a dog show

bred (BRED) mated dogs from specific breeds to produce pups with certain characteristics

breed (BREED) a kind of dog

brindle (BRIN-duhl) a mixture of dark and light hairs arranged in rows or bands

canine freestyle (KAY-nine FREE-*stile*) a type of dance performed to music by an owner and his or her dog

carriages (KA-rij-iz) the way dogs stand, sit, and walk

chrysanthemum (kruh-SAN-thuh-muhm) a type of plant with a large flower that has many small petals

coats (KOHTS) the fur or hair on dogs or other animals

companion (kuhm-PAN-yuhn) an animal or person with whom one spends time

dewclaws (DOO-klawz) extra toenails above a dog's paw

disorder (diss-OR-dur) an illness that affects the mind or body

extinct (ek-STINGKT) when a kind of plant or animal has died out

grooming (GROOM-ing) keeping an animal neat and clean

kennel (KEN-uhl) a place where dogs or cats are raised, trained, and looked after

lapdogs (LAP-*dawgz*) small dogs that are able to be held in people's laps

litter (LIT-ur) a group of baby animals, such as puppies or kittens, that are born to the same mother at the same time

Ming dynasty (MING DYE-nuh-stee) a period in Chinese history (1368–1644) when a series of rulers from the same family governed the country

regal (REE-guhl) fit for a king or queen

royal (ROI-uhl) relating to kings, queens, princes, and princesses

service dog (SUR-viss DAWG) a dog that helps a person who has health problems with daily tasks

show dogs (SHOH DAWGZ) dogs that take part in dog shows

sidecar (SIDE-kar) a car attached to the side of a motorcycle

veterinarian (*vet*-ur-uh-NER-ee-uhn) a doctor who takes care of dogs and other animals

weaned (WEEND) when a baby animal is eating food other than its mother's milk

Bibliography

Tarbell, Marta. "The Little Shih Tzu Who Could." *The Watch* (Telluride, Colorado) (December 24, 2009).

White, Jo Ann. *Shih Tzu: Your Happy Healthy Pet*. Indianapolis, IN: Howell Book House (2005).

Wood, Deborah. *The Shih Tzu (Terra Nova Series)*. Neptune, NJ: TFH Publications (2006).

www.americanshihtzuclub.org

Read More

Hanson, Anders. *Shaggy Shih Tzu*. Edina, MN: Abdo Publishing Company (2009).

Larrew, Brekka Hervey. *Shih Tzus*. Mankato, MN: Capstone Press (2008).

Sucher, Jaime. *Shih Tzu: A Complete Pet Owner's Manual*. Happauge, NY: Barron's Educational Series (2000).

Learn More Online

To learn more about Shih Tzus, visit
www.bearportpublishing.com/LittleDogsRockII

Index

About the Author

Joyce Markovics is an editor, writer, and orchid collector. She would like to dedicate this book to Maxwell, a Shih Tzu whose companionship and indomitable spirit have captured the hearts of his human family.